I WANT TO KNOW

Are Aliens Real?

Portia Summers and
Dana Meachen Rau

Enslow Publishing
101 W. 23rd Street
Suite 240
New York, NY 10011
USA

enslow.com

Published in 2017 by Enslow Publishing, LLC
101 W. 23rd Street, Suite 240, New York, NY 10011

Library of Congress Cataloging-in-Publication Data

Names: Summers, Portia, author. | Rau, Dana Meachen, 1971– author.
Title: Are aliens real? / Portia Summers and Dana Meachen Rau.
Description: New York, NY : Enslow Publishing, 2017. | Series: I want to know | Includes bibliographical references and index.
Identifiers: LCCN 2016024699| ISBN 9780766082304 (library bound) | ISBN 9780766082281 (pbk.) | ISBN 9780766082298 (6-pack)
Subjects: LCSH: Extraterrestrial beings—Juvenile literature. | Unidentified flying objects—Juvenile literature. | Life on other planets—Juvenile literature.
Classification: LCC QB54 .S9244 2017 | DDC 001.942—dc23
LC record available at https://lccn.loc.gov/2016024699

Printed in China

To Our Readers: We have done our best to make sure all websites in this book were active and appropriate when we went to press. However, the author and the publisher have no control over and assume no liability for the material available on those websites or on any websites they may link to. Any comments or suggestions can be sent by email to customerservice@enslow.com.

Photo Credits: Cover © iStockphoto.com/AidarZ; pp. 3, 27 Science Picture Co/Collection Mix: Subjects/Getty Images; p. 5 Robert Gendler/Science Photo Library/Getty Images; p. 6 Martin Bernetti/AFP/Getty Images; p. 7 nicolesy/E+/Getty Images; p. 8 Time Life Pictures/The LIFE Picture Collection/Getty Images; p. 9 Frank Zullo/Science Source/Getty Images; p. 11 Popperfoto/Getty Images; p. 12 Dennis van de Water/Shutterstock.com; p. 13 Art Montes De Oca/The Image Bank/Getty Images; p. 14 Heritage Images/Hulton Archive/Getty Images; p. 17 Daniel A. Leifheit/Moment/Getty Images; p. 18 New York Daily News Archive/Getty Images; p. 19 Noorullah Shirzada/AFP/Getty Images; p. 20 The Washington Post/Getty Images; p. 22 Loop Images/Universal Images Group/Getty Images; p. 23 Universal History Archive/Universal Images Group/Getty Images; p. 24 Getty Images; p. 26 Sherri Lynn Herrmann/EyeEm/Getty Images; p. 29 Stocksnapper/Shutterstock.com.

Contents

Chapter 1

Are We Alone?

Our planet is home to many types of animals and plants. The oceans, mountains, and forests of Earth are filled with life. More than seven billion people live on Earth now! In our solar system, Earth is the only planet that supports life. Scientists have found no other planets thus far that have life in any form—plants, insects, or even **bacteria**. However, some people think that there is life on other planets far outside our solar system, or even our **galaxy**.

Visitors from Another Planet

If there are living creatures, they may be able to think and act like we humans do. We call them aliens. The word "alien" means someone or something from a foreign place. Another planet certainly would be a foreign place! Many people tell stories about aliens coming to Earth.

In some stories, the aliens come to Earth to learn about humans and to share what they know. In other stories, these creatures come to take over Earth and destroy humans. Scientists don't think aliens have come to Earth yet. But there are many people who disagree. They think aliens have been landing on Earth for a very long time.

There are billions and billions of stars in space. There could be just as many, if not more, planets. And some of those planets could be home to aliens!

Cave paintings in Australia seem to show pictures of aliens. Some Egyptian hieroglyphs look like they depict aliens and **UFO**s. Some people think that some of the more amazing sites on Earth were created with the help of aliens. The heads on Easter Island, the Nazca Lines in Peru, and even the Egyptian pyramids have been credited to aliens. This theory is called the "ancient alien theory."

Because the Nazca Lines in Peru couldn't be seen until the invention of the airplane, giving humans a view from the sky, many people thought they were created by aliens as runways for UFOs landing on Earth.

Alien Appearances

No one can agree about what an alien from another planet might look like. Some say they are short with green skin. Others say that have large heads and gray skin. Still others say they have black eyes and long fingers. Maybe they are tall and thin? Maybe they look like insects! Or maybe they look just like you!

Imagine That!

Some researchers say that somewhere on the planet every three minutes, a UFO is spotted!

7

Messages from Earth

The *Voyager I* and *Voyager II* spacecraft are floating around the **universe**, taking photos and sending them back to Earth. But these spacecraft are also carrying messages from Earth, just in case they encounter alien life. Called the Golden Record, these images and recordings are supposed to tell aliens about humans and what our life is like on Earth. There are clips of sounds like heartbeats, laughter, crickets chirping, a train, and a kiss between mother and child. There are also recordings of music, including Beethoven, Bach, and Chuck Berry, as well as folk music from Mexico, Navajo tribes, Scotland, Senegal, and Zaire.

The universe is huge. We live in the Milky Way galaxy, which has hundreds of billions of stars. There are hundreds of billions of galaxies beyond ours. Scientists think that there are other living things out there. So they keep searching.

Scientists watch the skies using powerful telescopes that help them see thousands of miles away.

Chapter 2

. . . .

Unusual, Unexplained, and Unidentified

Tunguska [toong-GOO-skuh], Siberia, is a quiet town in northern Russia. In June 1908, however, a huge explosion in the sky shook the ground for 800 square miles (2,000 square kilometers). It ripped down millions of trees. Thankfully, the area is not heavily populated. However, it knocked people off their feet for miles around. No one knew what caused the blast, but eyewitnesses remember hearing what sounded like gunfire and seeing a bright column of bluish light in the sky.

Strange Sightings

In 1947, residents of Roswell, New Mexico, reported seeing strange lights in the sky. A short time later, a rancher found some strange wreckage on his land. Experts from the nearby Roswell Army Air Field came out to **investigate**. After the incident, the area became known as Area 51. Many years later, one of those experts said the crash had been an alien spaceship.

People who claim to have seen aliens often report bright lights, strange sounds, and even disappearing animals.

UFO sightings are the most common experience people claim to have with aliens.

In March 1966, more than one hundred people saw something unusual in Michigan. Lights darted and flashed through the sky for hours. Even police officers saw them. One officer tried to chase a light with his police car, but the lights vanished just as quickly as they had appeared.

Crop Circles

Some people think that crop circles are more **evidence** of aliens visiting Earth. Crop circles are strange shapes created in the crops in fields. The crops are bent over, which makes odd patterns in the field. These crop circles can really be seen only from the air, and they have been reported all over the world. No one really knows what causes them, but many people think it is aliens.

These are just three examples of UFO sightings. Some people believe unidentified flying objects are spaceships that are carrying aliens to Earth.

People still claim to see UFOs today. Some witnesses see bright flashes of light that fly across the sky impossibly fast. Others describe bright lights that disappear as soon as you look at them directly. Some see round, flat objects that hover over the ground.

Others report small objects that move quickly back and forth. They might move quietly. Or they may make a sizzling sound.

Abduction Experiences

Some people claim they have met aliens face to face. These people say they have been **abducted** by aliens and have spent time in their spaceships before being put back on Earth. The reason for these abductions isn't clear. Some say the aliens wanted to talk to them, while others claim the aliens wanted to study humans. Some people were frightened by their experiences, while others would love to go back with the aliens.

Chapter 3

. . . .

Aircraft or Flying Saucers?

Not everyone thinks UFOs are alien spaceships. The people who do believe say they have proof, such as photos or videos. Some of these photos are real. Others have proved to be fake. Many people really do see lights in the sky. But not all of them are UFOs.

Natural Explanations

Earth is a strange place. The northern and southern lights are colorful, moving lights in the sky. Ball lightning is a type of lightning that looks like a glowing white, blue, or orange ball. It hisses and seems to float in the sky. Maybe people have mistaken these lights for UFOs.

Scientists have determined that a space invader did cause the explosion in 1908 in Tunguska. A huge asteroid became overheated as it fell to Earth. It exploded into fiery pieces before it fell to the ground.

The northern lights, or aurora borealis, is a phenomenon of light that occurs in the extreme Northern and Southern Hemispheres.

War of the Worlds

In the 1930s, there was no television. People got much of their news and entertainment from radio. **Radio dramas** were especially popular. One of the most famous radio dramas aired on October 30, 1938. Orson Welles's *The War of the Worlds* was a fake news broadcast that was about aliens invading Earth. It was so convincing that many people believed it was real! They called their friends and family, newspapers and radio stations, thinking that the world was ending.

Technology in the Skies

People may see ships in the sky, but aliens don't always fly them. Technology has come a long way over the last hundred years. Scientists are developing new ways to travel all the time. And the US Air Force has drones, as well as other secret planes, that are fast, quiet, and hard to see. If someone sees one of these strange planes, they might think it is a UFO.

The wreckage found in 1947 in Roswell was most likely from a downed government or military experiment. Scientists had probably sent equipment high into the air using balloons. No one knows for sure what people saw over Michigan in 1966. The bursts of light could have

Drones are used by the US Air Force every day.

been caused by swamp gas. When plants in swampy places let off gas, it can catch fire.

Most UFOs turn out to be airplanes, balloons, meteors, or even birds! However, some UFOs really are unidentified and have no explanation. Maybe they really are aliens coming to visit!

Scientists watch the skies using powerful telescopes that help them see thousands of miles away.

Chapter 4

· · · · · · · · · ·

Seeking Life Among the Stars

Most scientists do not think that Earth is the only planet that supports life. Using very high-tech equipment, they are always searching for other planets that might have life. They, like us, wonder what alien life might be like and where it might be found.

Searching the Sky

Some scientists use **radio telescopes** to search the sky. Radio waves cannot be seen and travel very fast. This is what we use when we listen to the radio. They are capable of travelling through space. Radio telescopes pick up these waves. Scientists use these radio telescopes to search for changes or patterns in the usual radio waves from space. That might mean an alien is sending us a signal. If aliens were trying to talk with us, radio waves might be a good way to hear them.

Radio telescopes search for unusual radio waves, which may signal attempted communication from aliens.

Earth's Most Famous Aliens

Humans are fascinated with the idea of aliens from other planets. There have been many movies, books, and works of art about aliens. Some of Earth's more famous stories about aliens are:

- *The X-Files*
- *Dr. Who*
- *Star Wars*
- *Star Trek*
- *Close Encounters of the Third Kind*
- *Guardians of the Galaxy*
- *ET*
- *Alf*
- *Mork & Mindy*
- *Superman*

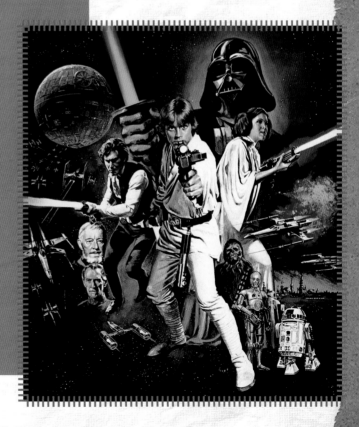

Other scientists are looking for life of simpler sorts, like plants, animals, and especially bacteria. They are searching for planets that have elements like oxygen, carbon dioxide, and a temperature that isn't too hot or too cold. Perhaps the most important element

It has recently been proved that there was once water on Mars. Water is one of the elements needed to support life.

scientists are looking for, however, is water. Life on Earth needs water to survive. Scientists **hypothesize** that water might be the key to life on any planet.

In 2015, scientists discovered that sometimes water flows on Mars. They also discovered that a global ocean is beneath the icy crust of Saturn's moon Enceladus. There is also a possibility that water might be under the layers of ice on Europa, a moon of Jupiter's.

Imagine That!

Aliens have been the subject of stories for thousands and thousands of years. In the second century, Roman writer Lucian wrote *True Fictions*, which is considered the first science-fiction story. In it, he talked about travelling to outer space, encountering aliens, and even robots! In the tenth century, *Tale of the Bamboo Cutter*, about a princess from the moon, was written in Japan. There are even stories about aliens in *1,001 Arabian Nights*!

Inconclusive Evidence

There are many possible explanations for aliens and encounters with them. Some people think that abductions are merely **hallucinations**. And many think that mysterious UFOs could be **mirages** or tricks of the eye. But there are just as many people who believe that

Aliens visiting Earth is something that is often discussed in TV, films, books, and stories. But many people believe it is more than fiction and that if aliens have not already visited us, they will soon.

aliens have visited us and continue their search for life on other planets.

People will always wonder what aliens are like. As many stories as there are about aliens, there will be more. And scientists continue their search for life outside of Earth. Some day, we may discover aliens, and we won't have to search or wonder anymore. Until then, keep looking to the skies, and maybe you'll spot an alien who has been searching for us!

Words to Know

abducted Taken away forcibly.

bacteria Single-celled microorganisms that reproduce quickly, can cause chemical changes to an environment, and can cause disease.

evidence Available information or facts about a situation or event.

galaxy A large group of stars in outer space.

hallucination Something that is seen but that isn't actually there.

hypothesize To suggest a theory.

investigate To carry out research and pose questions about a particular topic or event.

mirage A trick of the eye that is caused by weather, temperature, or atmosphere.

radio drama A play performed on the radio.

radio telescope A tool scientists use to catch signals from outer space.

UFO Unidentified flying object.

universe All of outer space and everything in it.

Further Reading

Books:

Aguilar, David A. *Alien Worlds: Your Guide to Extraterrestrial Life*. Washington, DC: National Geographic Kids, 2013.

Aguilar, David A. *Space Encyclopedia: A Tour of Our Solar System and Beyond*. Washington, DC: National Geographic Kids, 2013.

Brake, Mark. *Alien Hunter's Handbook: How to Look for Extra-Terrestrial Life*. New York, NY: Kingfisher Publishing, 2012.

Carney, Elizabeth. *Planets*. Washington, DC: National Geographic Kids, 2012.

Websites:

Discovery Kids

discoverykids.com/articles/do-aliens-really-exist

Find out what the experts say!

Time Magazine

www.timeforkids.com/news/are-we-alone/203396

Read more about aliens.

Voyager/NASA

voyager.jpl.nasa.gov/spacecraft/goldenrec.html

Learn more about the Voyager spacecraft.

Index